STUCKEDUP!

A BreakThrough Path to Unstuck

Vickie Griffith

StuckedUp!
A BreakThrough Path to Unstuck

StuckedUp! A BreakThrough Path to Unstuck/ Vickie Griffith
1. Spirituality   2. Self Help   3. Mind Body Spirit

ISBN: 1463665342
ISBN-13: 9781463665340
Library of Congress Control Number: 2011911195
CreateSpace, North Charleston, SC

Editing by:
Deb Childs
www.DeborahWaltersChilds.com

BreakThrough
www.Break-Through.org

Vickie has the magical ability to take lessons from her own life and use them as a guide for the reader to navigate their own story, which in turn, allows them to move toward health, wholeness and happiness. Her brutal honesty and clear insight into the deeper and underlying meaning of the challenges in her formative years, help inform the reader about how to reach the same understanding with their own story. A must read for everyone seeking a higher spiritual connection to themselves and their higher power.

Sue Kindred
Woofs 'n Wags Magazine
Editor

Would you mind Reading the Draft of My Book? These are the words spoken to me at a NSA Virginia meeting, a few months back, by one of the women, Vickie Griffith, who has made a difference in my and so many other lives. Sure I said surprised and honored by her request.

When she emailed me the draft, I tried hard to read it on line but I just couldn't. I had to print it to be sure I could see and feel every word. All I could keep saying was **WOW Vickie**; **WOW** this is so powerful; **WOW; WOW**! I couldn't believe what I was reading. I felt so strongly about what I read, I tested a few sentences on two friends and they started talking right away about how they could relate to what Vickie had written.

She has been able to put into words what many of us feel or have felt at some point in our lives. You will not regret purchasing this book. I just hope you let Vickie know that we appreciate her sharing some of her deepest thoughts with us.

Vickie, I want to personally "Thank you" for always helping us take a fresh look at matters of the soul.
Peace and Joy,

Shirley T. Burke
Chief Encourager
Esteem Institute

StuckedUp! What an insightful read! This book will make a difference in your life. Teaching from her heart, Vickie exposes difficult experiences in her life to help you break through to "unstuck". If you are fed up and ready to find your path to purpose – read this book!

Deb Childs
Childs Communications
President and Author

Table of Contents

Part Two – Set ...

Part Three – Go...D?

Acknowledgments

First and foremost, I want to thank my husband, Terry, who supports my dreams in more ways than I can recognize him in the space I have here. It touches my heart to know how much you believe in me.

Our incredible son, Travis, is truly one of my spiritual teachers. Your dad and I are so proud of the man, husband, and father you are.

Our daughter-in-law, Ashley, inspires others with her daily practice of living in faith. And those two bright stars that warm our hearts, make us laugh, and keep our eyes open to the childlike wonder of life—our granddaughters, Hannah Riley and Harlow Annalise.

My mom, Pat Stahl—you are amazing and inspiring. You taught me that I could do anything and encouraged me to do so.

I am grateful for the support and encouragement of my dear friends, not only through the book creation process, but through the process of life:

Sue Kindred, for brightening my thesis with her fabulous images of the world to help turn it into a book. I wish my brain saw life in the images she sees.

Christine Walters, for inspiring me to be me, "Yes, And" enabling me to see the funny side of life.

The Abundance Mastermind Group—Susie Galvez, Smokie Sizemore, and Christine Walters—we have attracted some amazing opportunities during our six months together.

My Goals Group—Debbie Stocks, Brenda Dennis, and Pam Chanfrau—we have been together longer than can remember! I am honored and awestruck when I am in the presence of these brilliant women. They are not only successful in business, but each of them lives life with purpose. They truly understand that creating life experiences with family and friends is the most valuable contribution they can make in life.

Miss Shirley T. Burke, who said, "Oh, yes, you have to," after she read the rough draft of my thesis and encouraged me to turn it into a book. It is no wonder she holds the title of Chief Encourager in her business.

To my spiritual teacher, Lisa Marks, whose class I joined to learn about Science of Mind. We walked through five years together as she watched me resist, reject, and reflect on the teachings. Luckily, there was a bowl of chocolate nearby for consoling the soul.

To Dave Jones, my classmate during the last three years of our ministerial program—what an amazing example of manifestation he experienced on that Father's Day before graduation when a knock on his door brought home his children he had not seen in 12 years!

To my two business coaches, Rene Haines and Laura Posey—their expertise and confidence in my work continues to give me courage—not to mention, they both hold me accountable to achieve my vision.

To all the many friends who have traveled through my life. You have touched my life in many ways that has assisted me to grow and heal.

Finally—many thanks to Deb Childs whose edits helped turn my ministerial thesis into a real book.

Introduction

There is never one path that gets us to where we are meant to be in life. One trail shapes how we deal with relationships, another handles our career choices, and yet a different lane guides us to our choice in spirituality. These pathways may be completely separate from one another or intertwined like a plate of spaghetti. Some paths are as smooth as the wet sand on an unoccupied beach or as twisted as the above-ground roots along a tree-lined concrete walkway in the city. We have many choices and opportunities to change the direction we take, whether it is the path up a mountain or down to the sea. There may seem to be many false starts and do-overs and times when we think we are ready, only to find out we are not. However, there is a particular path that is right for you, and it is leading you to your destiny. You will know 'It' when you get there.

I knew I'd reached my significant point of 'Ready' when I discovered what I had been searching for. After five years of classes, papers, lectures, and speeches, I had not arrived at 'Go', but I had finally made it to 'Set'. And with the skills and action steps learned in this 'study hall of life,' I quickly propelled past 'Go', while taking pleasure in the adventures of learning what was just beyond 'Go' for me.

"I am always ready to learn although I do not always like being taught."

Winston Churchill

1

What the...?

'Ready, Set, Go'! That famous starting phrase for so many childhood games became the phrase that defined my life … because, unfortunately, I got stuck at 'Ready'.

Flash back to a pregnant woman in labor at a southern military hospital. The delivery is progressing normally, but when it's time to start pushing, the doctor is MIA—Missing In Action. About fifteen minutes after a frantic, panicked phone call from the hospital staff, the doctor flings open the door to the delivery room so hard that it hits the back wall. A tall, burly man dressed in wild, plaid golf knickers and a green knit, collared shirt stomps into the room, visibly upset. This untimely delivery has pulled him away from the best game he'd ever played. Determined to get back to his game in as short a time frame as possible, the doctor grabbed the forceps and yanked the baby out. No coaxing or gentle encouragement … just grab, yank, and pull—and off he went, back to his important golf game.

Suddenly the newborn found itself thrust into a world she wasn't prepared to meet. No choice, no softness, no peeking out at her own pace. She was robbed of the experience of making her way to 'Ready'. She was just plopped there—in a new, cold, and unwelcoming place where she had no desire to be.

You guessed it. That newborn was me, and subsequently, my whole life has felt like it's been about not being ready. No amount of planning, studying, visualization, or practice has allowed me to feel anything but unprepared. I stalled, avoided, and even evaded change. Where others seem to move smoothly forward, I stuttered and held back. I felt like I was just waiting for someone to say, "You are ready," and pull me into action.

After many decades, when I finally found myself sitting across from someone who could be that person, I questioned whether a teacher or mentor was what I was looking to find. Could this really be what or who I needed to coax, prod, and nudge me into moving way past 'Ready', maybe even all the way to 'Go.' And if I got to 'Go,' would I have everything I needed to finally be ready? Little did I know that getting to 'Go' meant meeting and understanding God.

Skeptical about any type of formalized religion and the presumption of accompanying rituals, I hesitated. What if this path was the same, old religion I grew up with? My heart, however, yearned for validation and expressed a need for confirmation of my belief systems. Soft inner whispers hinted to me that there was more to this earthly playing field than I consciously understood. Unbeknownst to me, the Universe was initiating the baby steps I needed to take to feel prepared for 'Go.' And spirituality happened to be an important part of that path. But before I realized where I was going, there was a heavy dose of life and rocky paths to deal with along the way.

Opportunities for Growth

Have you ever felt stuck? Trapped, not ready?

Our paths are rarely straight and clear. In fact, they are usually crooked, rocky, and full of forks. Often there are persons or events that show up on your path that feel like roadblocks to keep you stuck amongst the knotty roots of the road. In actuality, they are there to propel you forward in the right direction.

You may remember some who pushed you and those who aggravated you. Others probably praised and supported you. But in some way they helped you move forward, to get unstuck. Many times, they activated a shift in your smallest actions or baby steps.

Contemplate

Who in your life propelled you forward? Think back. Can you recognize them now for the role they had in getting you to your destination? These guides may have been acquaintances, co-workers, family, friends, or a casual contact that showed up out-of-the-blue with unexpected and uncanny information.

Action Step

Make a list of the ten most important or memorable people who have impacted your life. Whether the situation involving them was uncomfortable or encouraging, these people were brought into your life to keep you on the path or shift you to your purpose.

"You will decide on a matter and it will be established for you, and a light will shine on your way."

Job 22.28

(Kings James Version Holy Bible)

2

The Stress of Recess

A first-grade girl stands by herself against the side of the elementary school building watching the other children play during recess. Alone and hovering on the edge of all the activity, this is her usual place to stand and watch. Rarely is she invited to join in. No jump rope, kick ball, or swinging with the other children—all because she looks different. The adults use euphemisms such as heavy, husky, or overweight to describe her. The kids just call her fat. Every day she hears the same old rhyme … "Fatty, fatty, two by four … can't get through the kitchen door." Even when the kids aren't singing it out loud, she can still hear it in her head.

She observes and watches their actions and listens to their words. In her mind she wonders, "Why did Johnny say that? What makes Billy so mean? Why is Darcie so popular?" Sometimes the pieces would come together, and she could see the puzzle picture, and sometimes it just didn't make sense.

Even at such a young age, down in the quiet center of her heart, this child knew that all the hurtful words being thrown her way were only a reflection of the pain inside her tormentors. Something inside made them feel inferior and afraid to think independently of what they'd been told.

She wanted to fit in and be accepted more than anything. But somehow she knew that if she fell into their pattern of behavior, being mean and hateful, unkind and unfriendly, it would hurt her more than it was worth. She accepted them as they were.

I was that little girl on the playground. Discovering the power I held within was also many decades away. The observational skills I learned growing up as 'the fat girl' formed the very core of the foundation that helps my business practice flourish today. I now realize that I was attuned to the Divine Law of Cause and Effect, even before I knew it existed and at an age that would normally defy understanding it.

The old saying "what goes around comes around" espouses the idea that any thought or action that we create comes back to us, multiplied. This is true whether the effects are helpful or hurtful—or as a cause of reason, motive, or occasion. As further explained by Ernest Holmes, "Causation, too, is the act or agency by which an effect is produced, and Effect is that which did not make itself, but which must have a power back of it causing it to be."

Since the law travels in both directions, striking back at those kids would not have produced the desired outcome of fitting in. Eventually, they did stop their badgering and teasing. Did I ever fit in? Not really. But I did have a stillness inside that made me know I was okay.

Opportunities for Growth

She wanted to fit in and be accepted more than anything. But somehow she knew that if she fell into their pattern of behavior—being mean and hateful, unkind and unfriendly—it would hurt her more than it was worth. She accepted them as they were.

I was that little girl on the playground. Discovering the power I held within was also many decades away. The observational skills I learned growing up as 'the fat girl' formed the very core of the foundation that helps my business practice flourish today. I now realize that I was attuned to the Divine Law of Cause and Effect even before I knew it existed and at an age that would normally defy understanding it.

The Law of Cause and Effect is always working for you. It always says yes to your requests and brings them back to you. These requests go out from you in the form of your thoughts, beliefs, behaviors, or intentions.

How has this happened to you? If you examine particular situations that came to bear, you may discover that you had thoughts or feelings about yourself that brought those events to life. Every day you make choices and form opinions about life experiences or feelings, and the effects of those thoughts and choices come back to you in a myriad of ways. It can seem like a vicious cycle until you realize who's in charge.

A well-educated, attractive, young professional woman sought my assistance in attracting a fulfilling relationship. She was attracting men who were emotionally unavailable, and often married. All treated her unkindly. She continued to attract this type of man until she dealt with her self-esteem issues stemming from childhood. Once she started taking care of herself—including her body, home, and car—she started attracting men who wanted to be with her. Her inner feelings of low self-worth were causing the effect of attracting the wrong types of relationships to her.

Contemplate

What experiences or people are you bringing into your life that keep reminding you of your deep-seeded belief system about yourself and who you are?

Action Step

Look at your list from Chapter One. Write the one word beside each person that describes the primary feeling you had as a result of your experience with them. Write one sentence describing the belief about yourself that your experience with that person confirmed.

Examples of this are: I am not good enough. I am not smart enough. My body is not the way I want it. Or perhaps you thought: I can achieve anything I want. These are your feelings, and they do not make you right or wrong. Nor do they mean you will feel that way about your self forever. You are an ever-growing and changing person who wants the most out of your life. You would have never picked up this book if that were not true.

Action Step

If the belief that you developed in the exercise above is a negative one, write down a positive statement that you would rather believe about your self. It is okay if you don't believe it is possible for now. On your journey through reading this book, you will discover how to make the changes necessary to erase those old daunting belief systems so that you are using the Law of Cause and Effect to your advantage.

Action Step

Read the positive statements you have affirmed every night just prior to sleep to reprogram your subconscious mind.

"We stand today on the edge of a new frontier - the frontier of the 1960's – a frontier of unknown opportunities and perils - a frontier of unfulfilled hopes and threats."

John F. Kennedy

3

Peace, Love, and Paper Cut-Outs

A young girl sits on her bedroom floor with scraps of colored construction paper spread across the carpet before her. She has been working for hours, cutting out letters and doves and shaping different colors of the scrap paper into beautiful flower petals.

The project was her idea. She had a driving motivation to finish it; she wanted to create a masterpiece, much like Michelangelo's Sistine Chapel—even though she didn't know what or where the Sistine Chapel was. It was just a name in a story she'd heard.

This masterpiece she created for her bedroom ceiling revealed her desires for the world—Hope, Love, Peace, and Brotherhood. A multi-hued rainbow of letters, each one eight inches tall, spelling out the dream of "Botherhood." That's right—Botherhood; it seems she had forgotten the "R," and with its absence came a message that was even more powerful. While the young girl felt bothered by the war, mistrust, drugs, hate, predictions of doom, she was still able to trust in the promise and hope of brotherhood—the word she had meant to spell.

As clear as an eight-year-old could be—a message that came from somewhere deep inside; an understanding, a knowing, a glimpse of the future. We are 'One.' We can create change for the better. We have the power to make a difference in our lives and in the lives of others. And on that day, she had made a difference on the ceiling in her bedroom.

I am that little girl — a product of the 60s. My first decade on the earth is synonymous with ideas of the new, exciting, radical, and rebellious events and trends sweeping across the country at that time. The many trials and tribulations during the daze of craze brought with them a feeling of tension and unrest.

The Vietnam War, coupled with radical and rampant discrimination, created a fervent desire for women to want, and to loudly demand, more visibility and independence. The time even gave birth to a new surname for women—Ms. This generation wanted nothing more than to break free of the social constraints of a previous, more restrained and restrictive generation.

The era was identified by slogans like "Make love not war," "peace and flower power." Popular TV shows like The Smothers Brothers Comedy Hour, Red Skelton, and The Mod Squad provided escapism and a relief from the tensions of the day. Many young people turned to drugs as another way to escape.

Even with all of the tension, struggles, and strife growing up during this era felt right to me. Loving one another just made sense. I didn't understand exactly what was right or wrong about it, but I knew the war and the expressions of hatred fostered by the media coverage of the war were not the way I wanted to feel. I leaned toward feeling connected to others and felt that as a generation, we could set ourselves free from the expectations of our forbearers.

The events of this decade helped shape me. Somehow, ahead of my time, I knew that we all had the right to express ourselves, just as it was our right to do more, have more, and to BE more. And though I did not understand the concept of us all being One, I can see why I chose this era to begin my journey of knowing that I am part of the Divine and One with all.

Opportunities for Growth

Fear thrusts us out of Grace with the union with God. Fear was a constant state of emotion when I was growing up in the 1960's. Riots, protest, and distrust of the young generation created horror over anything that was different. During times of trouble, we form momentary lapses of forgetfulness that God is our Source of all that is. Everything in the Universe, this world, is made of God.

Therefore, you too, are part of the Divine. And as hard as it is to believe, so are the people of your past that hurt you in some way. We neglect to remember our true nature of being part of God, and that we have the spirit of God dwelling within us. Everyone does.

The bible states, "So God created man in his own image, in the image of God created he him; male and female, created he them." *King James 2000 Bible (©2003)*

It does not say that you, Margaret, were created in the image of God but Betty, your best friend who stole your money, is not. She, too, was made in the image of God. Therefore, as painful as it may seem, we are all connected to God and to each other—even Betty.

The ego wishes that our oneness with each other was not true. It will do everything to separate us from each other. Yet, science is studying the spiritual and religious parts of our brains and making amazing discoveries in the possibility that our brains are hardwired to feel close to God. Scientifically and spiritually, we are finding that because we were made in the image of the Creator, we are all one.

There may be good reason to get over that hurt and pain someone has caused you. If you have not thrown the book across the room at this point and are still reading, something inside of you knows this to be true.

Contemplate

Look at your list of ten people. Did the experience with them help you to feel closer to God or more separate from God? If you imagine them as a Divine image of God, in their *unique* way, can you see them differently? Can you feel differently about the situation involving them?

Action Step

Acknowledge your feelings about your list of ten people. Are you still mad, sad, or resentful? Do you feel guilty, want to blame them, or _____ (insert your feelings here)? It is perfectly okay to have those feelings.

There is nothing wrong with any feeling. What harms us as our need to harbor the negative emotions associated with the negative memory. This action is like taking poison and hoping the other person will die. Only you will be harmed in the end. So, for now, just notice your feelings about the list of ten, without judgment of whether it is right or wrong to feel this way.

"It is required of every man," the ghost returned, "that the spirit within him should walk abroad among his fellow-men, and travel far and wide; and, if that spirit goes not forth in life, it is condemned to do so after death."

A Christmas Carol, Charles Dickens

4

Who Is Here?

Growing up, my family and I lived in an older home with elegant floor registers. Those were the vents through which the heat flowed to keep the house warm. They were the really old-fashioned kind, with decorative black filigree coverings, and the kind that held secret noises and whispered conversations that curious little girls could hear if they listened quietly.

Sometimes I would crouch on the floor of my second-story bedroom, press my ear against the heating vent and strain to hear the conversations around the kitchen table directly below my room. On one particular night when I was eight, my parents were having a conversation with a guest that was scary, intriguing, and a little overwhelming.

I hung on every word, straining to hear their lowered voices and whispered thoughts, catching only every third word, but every bit of their tension and fear. They were telling stories about spirits, ghosts, and apparitions. I knew … just knew … that these invisible energies could snatch me away.

Would they visit me? What would they want from me? Would they be scary and mean, and would I be able to see them coming for me? Were they watching me now, judging my every move like Santa Clause … knowing if I was naughty or nice? What would they do if I was naughty?

The more I heard, the more frightened I became. When I absolutely couldn't take any more, I ran back to my bed, jumped smack in the middle, and pulled the covers over my head. The safety net I created with my covers offered a sense of protection to me from the ghosts I thought might be in my room.

All of my eight-year-old wisdom told me I couldn't talk to my parents about my fears … they would tell me how silly I was and send me back to bed with a pat and a smile. But, while I knew I couldn't talk about spirits and unseen things that prattle around under the cover of darkness, I also knew that I needed something to protect me. So I cleverly and wisely created a bubble of loving protection by surrounding myself with every single one of my stuffed animals and dolls. My bed piled high with my protectors and clutching my Raggedy Ann doll, I fell into a deep, restful sleep that first scary night. I recreated this ritual of safety and protection every night for years.

Every morning when I would wake, all of the stuffed animals would be scattered all over the floor. I believed they came to life after I fell asleep, and they would play and dance while protecting me until the morning came. And much like in the movie, *Toy Story*, as dawn approached, they became loose and limp and turned into toys once more, yet standing ready to serve me again the next night.

My conscious child-mind may not have known exactly how I was being protected, but my subconscious mind did know I would have protection whenever I needed it. I always seemed to have a sense of the Divine … a guidance I could call upon to help me create a web of safety, protection, and the knowledge that there was something bigger and more powerful than me, my parents, or any ghost or ghoul.

Opportunities for Growth

My conscious child-mind may not have known exactly how I was being protected, but my subconscious mind knew I would have protection whenever I needed it. I always seemed to have a sense of the Divine … a guidance I could call upon to help me create a web of safety, protection, and the knowledge that there was something bigger and more powerful than me, my parents, or any ghost or ghoul.

What form of protection did you create for yourself as a child?

Patty grew up in volatile home. Her parents where constantly fighting. Loudly and forcibly, their words cut into her as deeply as if they were throwing knives at her. Even though she was not at fault, she felt responsible for the problems her parents had, as all children do. There was no one that she trusted. She felt alone, and there she could not express her fears. So instead, she turned to food. Food comforted her as her parents threw blame and insults at each other. Food helped her to escape the chaos for a moment or two. Plumping up her body enabled her to create a wall of safety around her.

Twenty five years later with a full time job, two small children, and a husband that cherishes her, she is still overweight. Even now she uses food to comfort her during stressful times, to protect her during times of conflict.

But, she has come to the realization that the dysfunctional habit of eating for protection is no longer serving her. She has sense recognized that a Higher Source is available for refuge and she is incorporating the practice of calling on that Source for guidance and protection. She is allowing herself to feel one with the safety and refuge of the Divine, while releasing old fears through Hypnosis and Emotional Freedom Techniques.

Contemplate

What dysfunctional habits have you created for protection from childhood? Note the habit of perfectionism is also a protection mechanism. Do you eat, smoke, or drink to soothe your emotions during stressful times? Do you overspend on material goods to avoid facing a major loss you once suffered?

Action Step

Make a list of five habits you would like to release. What emotions do they evoke? How is your habit serving you now?

"Life is not meant to be easy, my child; but take courage – it can be delightful."

George Bernard Shaw

5

This Should Be Easy

No one promised anything would be easy. I believe that prior to our arrival in this realm, we contract to follow a path that will allow us to achieve a pre-chosen goal. We cannot fail. But, no one promised it would be easy to succeed.

Thirteen is a hard age under the best of circumstances. At the peak of my 'tween years, my parents separated for about a year to work on their marriage. As with any child, I internalized my emotional trauma and felt unloved and alone. I coped with these feelings by losing a lot of weight and seeking approval in the guise of a boyfriend. And an even bigger guise—love; well, it looked like love at the age of 13.

He was 16 and in high school. I was an eighth-grade, middle school student. It was amazingly cool to be dating a high school boy! I hung out with other high school kids at a friend's house every night, and occasionally we would scoot over to the big town of Lansing and cruise around the Capitol of Michigan. It was a tremendous relief to feel loved and away from the trauma of my home life.

I don't remember my first kiss, like most young women do. Instead, I remember my first "almost kiss." It was a quiet, warm spring evening, and we were on the front porch of my girlfriend's house. I would need to be home very soon, so we stepped outside to be alone. Facing each other, we slowly leaned in close — all puckered up for that romantic first kiss. Just as our lips were about to meet, my girlfriend shoved open the screen door and shouted, "Hey, what are you guys doing?" We separated quickly, and in unison stammered, "Ah, nothin'."

I'm sure we did have that first kiss at some point, but the events of a few months later pushed all memories of my first 'love' out of my conscious mind. In fact, every pleasant memory of him was obliterated when he raped me in my own home. It was a day when I was sick and stayed home from school. He played hooky to stay with me, and I remember thinking how sweet it was for him to stay with me, even though I was sick. But, the sweetness in that thought turned bitter and as ugly and sick as I felt inside.

I never told my parents — just like I never told them about the ghosts I was afraid of. They had their own problems to deal with, and I wasn't about to call their attention back to me and my problems. So, I repressed the memory and pretended it never happened.

My teenage years continued to be miserable. I found it very difficult trying to figure out who I was, who I wanted to be, and who I thought I should be. By the time I was fifteen, my parents had reconciled and slowly, the pounds I had lost began to return. As I got heavier and heavier, I also became more and more depressed. My parents were still having trouble with their marriage, and decided to move the family about an hour away from our hometown. I didn't mind moving so much—starting over couldn't be that bad when you weren't really happy where you were.

However, we moved to the most prestigious public high school district in the state of Michigan. This school could have been the template for the TV show 90210, where everyone was pretty or handsome, and skinny with good skin. These were some fashion-conscious, luxury-living, and good-looking kids. I wondered where in the world a reserved, fat teenager with pimples was supposed to fit in.

I did make some friends, but it still felt like living on the Island of Misfit Toys in a Rudolph, the Red-Nosed Reindeer, video. We were invisible to the "In" crowd. The cheerleaders and jocks would never acknowledge us, and no one would ever consider asking us for a date. Apparently moving away doesn't mean leaving your problems behind. I went into my junior year heavier than I'd ever been before, and my parents' relationship problems did not disappear either.

Fortunately, they did recognize my misery and unhappiness and found two people to help me. These two people provided the catalyst that would ultimately change my life.

Opportunities for Growth

You have had ups and downs in your life; moments that felt like time was standing still, others that were fleeting. We have all had beautiful moments, cherished moments, and awe-inspiring moments. But, if you are still breathing, I bet you have also had trying, difficult, heart-wrenching times in your life.

Your path may have felt at times as though it was unraveling right before your eyes. There seemed to be nowhere to go. You would have liked to have a choice, but there were no forks in the road to choose between. No bench at the side of the road for a much deserved break. In fact, sometimes it feels like the path is leading you right off a cliff. At times in your life the path may not have been easy or simple, but you made it through. Life went on.

The experience with the "boyfriend" I trusted to respect my boundaries and my feelings altered my concept of myself and sent me inward to be alone again. But, eventually I came out stronger than before and my negative experience with him put me on a path that influenced my career in a way that would enable me to help others in ways I never could have imagined without the experience. From the pain of my own self discovery, I now help free others from the negative influences from abuse and more.

Contemplate:

No doubt, someone or something happened to divert your course along the way to shift you to the path you are presently on or to the path you needed to take to create your higher purpose. Think back to your list of ten people who impacted your life. Did the experience you had with any of them influence the course of your path?

Action Step

List one meaningful example in your life of a way that someone on your list knocked you off your path to create a new one or make you more determined to stay on the path you where on?

"You have power over your mind - not outside events. Realize this, and you will find strength."

Marcus Aurelius

6

Sweet 16

We journey through our lives, moving from one experience to another. Navigating the ebb and flow of treacherous waters, we think that every event is unrelated to the one before it, and the one that follows. Yet, when reflection lends awareness to the way our life has unfolded, we discover that the path we were traveling was well-marked after all.

When I was younger and in the moment, I didn't worry about what might be around the corner, whether it was good or bad or how it might affect me in the future. Now, looking back on the process and progress of my life, I realize that at the sweet age of 16, I was introduced to my future career…twice!

The first person to help lead me down the road to my future path was a chiropractor who had just developed a program for weight loss through hypnosis.

My parents signed me up, and I was excited to try it. I thought if I could just lose the weight, I would become popular like I had been at age 13 when I was thin. I knew well enough from that time in my life, that being thin didn't solve all of life's problems. But I thought it would at least give me a fighting chance to fit in as I aimed for acceptance in the '90210 Land of Beautiful People.'

And lose weight I did—30 pounds! But, unfortunately, I didn't keep it off. The hypnosis only addressed the diet part of losing weight; the effect of the problem was remedied, but the cause of it was not. Lying deep underneath the extra pounds was an inability to handle the emotional issues of my life.

No one has ever attributed my weight problems growing up to the psychological trauma I may have experienced in my journey through the birth canal and my rushed entry into the world. But those types of births have been connected to emotional insecurities and fearfulness in children. It makes me wonder if the doctor's golf game really did set the tone for my life! In any event, my weight problems started in early childhood. I was a very fat toddler, child, and teenager. As the years passed, I got heavier and heavier, and more depressed as time went on. I was then, and still experience being, an emotional eater.

But in my ability to lose 30 pounds through hypnosis, I found something far more valuable than weight loss — I found hope for the very first time. I became intrigued by the power of the mind. I realized that I did have something powerful and unique in me after all. I had discovered a tool that could help me reach my goals. I knew then that I could be different from others and still feel good about myself. What a concept!!

I began to study hypnosis in every way I could. I took classes and wrote papers on the subject. I was hooked. I still didn't expect that later in my life, hypnosis would become my career.

The second person my parents sent me to was a psychologist and a really cool, older dude. He was probably the age I am now, but at fifteen, I considered him an old dude—although, a cool one. Our appointments together were safe and comfortable. I told him everything, including my anger at my parents and how I felt disgustingly fat and unlovable. He helped me understand that I am more than my body. Long before Nike used the slogan as a brand, he told his patients, "Just do it!" He gave me tools that I still use today when I am afraid of stepping out in a new direction.

He taught me the value of "fake it until you make it." This practice serves me well, even today. It simply involves pretending and projecting confidence in whatever scares me most, while repeating a new action or habit over and over again. Soon that new confident pattern occurs without any conscious thought or feelings of fear. Many people think I am adventurous in my life and career. They see me as comfortable and confident. But, the truth is that often I am just pretending. I know that the practice of pretending is the second step in changing, and I am halfway there. The first step of change is visualization, which is a huge part of hypnosis.

While working with the psychologist, the story finally came up about my last boyfriend. I had been so successful in burying the bad memory that I couldn't even remember his name. I do remember that I denied he raped me. At our next session, we used hypnosis to enable me to recall the repressed memory and accept the reality of what he had done. Many women who've been raped often feel responsible for the event, and I was no exception. Through hypnosis, I was able to address my feelings and forgive myself.

Somehow I doubt that hypnosis was often used back then to help children with weight gain or other issues that concerned their parents. There is still a lack of awareness about the benefits of hypnosis today, decades later. So, looking back, it is now very obvious to me that my life was pre-ordained in a way that exposed me to the healing powers of hypnosis. The opportunity to experience hypnosis became a stepping stone on my spiritual path to the study of the Science of Mind, a religious philosophy. Through it, I was guided to an awakening of my own Divine Essence.

I grew more curious about how the mind worked, and the more I learned, the more curious I became. As the path continued to unfold, I began to know and understand myself better. I came to realize that I was always more than just a child of God. I am a *part* of God, and that knowledge is infinitely more empowering.

As a result of the challenges placed before me and the special teachers who appeared to help me overcome them, I was firmly placed on the path to my future career; one that was especially designed for me. Yes, there were detours, pot holes and traffic jams along the way, but the path was always taking me in the right direction. And that direction eventually led me to the full awareness that I am a spiritual being — a gift for which I am ever grateful.

Opportunities for Growth

Hypnosis is defined as a heightened state of focus, concentration, and inner awareness. Usually, a state of calm relaxation within the body takes place while distractions are blocked out. This is a normal and natural state that our brains enter into every day, several times a day. Hypnosis can utilize the brain-wave state that studies have shown to be more receptive to suggestion. It feels like waking into consciousness in the morning without an alarm clock to shock you there.

You body is relaxed. Your mind is wondering what time it is, and whether or not you have time to go back to sleep. Not quite asleep; not quite awake—a time when you are aware of your surroundings, yet not ready to get up and be fully alert. Your brain goes in and out of these states throughout the day. You are most influenced by a hypnotist because your thoughts and beliefs are continuing to program your actions.

Hypnosis is used to gain control of destructive behaviors, habits, and emotions. The Mayo Clinic explains that hypnosis is used along with other therapies to help with a variety of medical conditions.

Hypnosis may be used for:

- Pain Control
- Smoking Cessation
- Stress Reduction Related to Medical Procedures
- Mental Health Conditions
- Allergies
- Asthma
- Surgical Preparation
- Childbirth
- Weight Loss
- Athletic Performance
- Dental Procedures

- Coping with Chemotherapy
- Skin Conditions
- Gastrointestinal Problems

Hypnosis is best known for its ability to help in moving past those times in our lives when we feel stuck and unable to move forward or make a decision. Visualizing vivid and meaningful mental images grooms the potential to reach our goals.

Some of the areas in your life that may be helped with hypnosis are:

- Trauma
- PSTD
- Self Esteem
- Self Confidence
- Memory and Concentration
- Phobia and Anxieties
- Emotional Blocks
- Overcoming Addictions
- Substance Abuse
- Psychosomatic Illnesses
- Changing Limiting Beliefs
- Compulsive Behavior
- Emotional Release
- Managing Stress
- Spiritual Attunement
- Releasing Unwanted Habits

Hypnosis creates an open awareness to suggestion, though you would never participate in a behavior against your will or faith. With practice, you will be able to induce self-hypnosis. Like any skill, it takes time to learn and become proficient in it.

The guidelines below will get you started. There are some experiences in our lives that will require professional help. Getting professional assistance will help you achieve your goal more efficiently in most cases and with much less emotional strain.

Contemplate

Consider a goal where tangible results will be self-evident for your first efforts with self-hypnosis.

Action Step

Choose one positive affirmation that is in alignment with your goal. If your goal is to lose weight, some of these examples are:

- I choose to eat three green vegetables a day.
- I feel calm and relaxed every day.
- I am healthy, flexible, and strong.
- I consume the right amount of calories for my ideal body weight.
- I love to move my body.
- Every day, in every way, I am getting better and better.

Action Step

Follow the steps below to learn and enjoy self-hypnosis:

- Keep your eyes focused on something across the room in a vague, dreamy way.
- Breathe in deeply through your nose.
- Exhale slowly through your nose.

Repeat this twice more.

- On the third exhale, close your eyes.
- Count backwards to yourself or out loud from 25 down to 1, repeating the word "calm" or "relaxed" after each number.

When you reach the number one, repeat your personal affirmation, either out loud or to yourself 10 times.

- Count your self back to a relaxed awareness by counting up from 1 to 10.
- At 10, open your eyes and repeat the words, "I am relaxed, yet revitalized."

Ahhhhh! Doesn't that feel good?

Action Step

Practice at least once a day for 30 days. Pay attention to your behaviors and your thoughts. Changes may be so subtle and easy that you may notice them.

"The first step toward change is awareness.
The second step is acceptance."

Dr. Nathaniel Branden

7

A Grooming Appointment

It's true that we are always being groomed to remember that we are spiritual beings. Even when we are going through upsetting and challenging times, we should always remember that we are spiritual. Just like a child learning to take their first steps, we do everything in a most difficult way. We require a cheering section and additional supervision. The angels and guides must look at us and shake their heads in amusement.

Looking back with 20:20 hindsight, I can see that my life experiences were placing me squarely on a path to self-acceptance and forgiveness. My teenage years were miserable. I was over 200 pounds and felt lonely, angry, and full of self-hatred. But I did have an angelic cheering section and was growing in my ability to take the leap of faith toward self-acceptance.

I now know that I have a binge-eating disorder. Binge eating is a learned coping mechanism that compels someone to eat large quantities of food without purging it. From the moment I got home from school, I would start grazing through the kitchen like a buffalo in a green meadow. I wouldn't stop until I went to sleep. And, I certainly wasn't filling up on carrots and celery sticks! Chips, pizza bites, canned ravioli and anything chocolate were my friends. But as soon as that first piece of food would hit my mouth, I would start in on myself with a barrage of negative self-talk. "What is wrong with you? Why are you doing this? You will always be fat. You are so weak. You can't do anything right!"

Of course, I would start a new diet every morning. But my diet would consist of fasting all day long, and by the time I got home from school, I was ravenous, and the whole eating cycle would start over again. Because I hated myself, I was usually upset about something I said or did, and that only fueled the binge-eating fire.

The tormented eating cycle served to keep me in a place of punishment. I didn't feel worthy of anything—certainly not to feel better, or do better, or have better. I wasn't worthy of love or respect. Not me. I was fat, and fat people don't deserve the good things in life, or so I thought. Until one day I happened across a magazine that showed me something different … a different view of fat women.

Growing up I loved to read. Books were my refuge. At least once a week I would ride my bike — the basket filled with library books — across town to swap out the old books for new stories. During my teen years when we lived just outside a university town, I could find respite inside the myriad of bookstores that graced every corner. I could forget about my misery and my weight and find a little spot of peace.

My epiphany came on a typical miserable day of school. I'd just received a "C" on an English paper and a "D" on an algebra test. None of my friends would sit with me at lunch, and so my first stop after school was the kitchen pantry. Stuffing my face with cans of ravioli, bags of potato chips and several dozen cookies, I miserably waited for my mom to get home with the car, so I could escape to the bookstore.

Calm descended upon me as I wandered through the aisles of the bookstore and made my way to the magazine section. The feel, the quiet, the smell … it was all a safe haven for me … for a little bit of time I was okay, and I could leave my wretched fat self behind in my mind.

Gazing along the magazine racks, I spied one I'd never seen before. It was different and it leaped out at me. A stunning, beautiful, and sexy woman looked out at me. And she was FAT!

She looked amazing, and not only was she FAT, she was on the cover of a magazine! Wow, I had no idea that fat women could look that gorgeous; let alone be the cover model for a magazine.

BBW, *Big Beautiful Women,* is a magazine devoted to helping above- average-sized women live happy, successful lives and to love themselves even though they are considered plus-sized. This magazine is dedicated to the fat acceptance movement. I didn't just read this magazine, I devoured it. For the first time in my memory, I was engaged in gulping up something other than food. This magazine encouraged me to be beautiful, regardless of my size. It gave me hope. It gave me the courage to believe that my life could be different, and that I was not destined to feel horrible about myself just because I was fat. I read about other women who were famous, successful, confident, and who just happened to also be FAT.

It's amazing to me that something as simple as a magazine changed my attitude about myself. That magazine helped me understand that I was more than I thought I was. I could learn how to accept myself even though I was fat. I realized I am worthy, loveable, and valuable. It was one more of the small steps of spiritual growth that further propelled me onto the Science of Mind path many years later.

Opportunities for Growth

Marcie is fifty, feisty, and fat. She wants to lose 25 pounds. Every diet she has ever been on worked.... for a while. She would lose 10 or 15 pounds until something unexpected happened, and then she would eat like a maniac again, gaining all, if not more, of the original weight back.

In chilling detail, she referred to herself as a fatty with no willpower. She told me how stupid she was because she knew how to diet. She had been doing it for years. She criticized herself and her efforts. She talked about how her body was flabby, saggy, lumpy, and just plain ugly.

When asked what happened to sabotage her last efforts. She replied, "A birthday party; it was my party. I wanted to let loose of the constraints of my diet and just live a little. I met some friends at my favorite restaurant. We wined and dined. The next day my sister invited me to a barbecue for my birthday. Every day for a week after, I used my birthday as an excuse to indulge. Every night I would look at myself in the mirror and tell myself how ugly I was, how disgusting I was that I could not control myself. How no one would ever love me because I was so fat. I gained 10 pounds and just gave up."

Ready to give it another try, she had purchased the "right foods." She had started to walk again for exercise. She assured me that she should be walking more, eating more vegetables, and cooking more for herself. Before she had even started on her new regimen, she was already bullying her efforts without realizing it. Nothing she was doing was good enough.

Her goal was to lose weight through her old methods of self-bullying, intimidation, harassment, tormenting, browbeating, and badgering. She stated that her methods worked for a while in the past, and she would lose weight. The question was, "Had she ever kept the weight off?" Sadly, the answer was, "NO!"

A new diet was incorporated this time—one with a healthy dose of self-acceptance. It would be a diet without negative self- talk, judgment, or criticism; a diet enriched with healthy, loving words and nurtured with recognition of worthiness, love, success, and value.

Contemplation

What have you been bullying yourself about? When you look at the list of the ten people who have impacted your life, do you hear the mini-bully step up to put you in your place? What would happen if you said instead, "I did the best I could, given the time and circumstances in my life?"

Action Step

Try that response for a change. Look into your eyes in the mirror and say to your self, 'I did the best I could, given the time and circumstances in my life. I deserve to feel loved, precious, and valued. I love you."

Do this three times a day, always looking in a mirror. Say this affirmation lovingly to the child within the person looking back at you and mean it.

"Give love and unconditional acceptance to those you encounter, and notice what happens."

Dr. Wayne Dyer

8

Tangled Rings

The decade of our twenties is all about self-discovery — learning who we are, where we are going, and exploring the bigger picture of our lives. I longed for the prince charming that every girl likely dreams of at some point in their imagined fairytale lives. I wanted him to come swiftly into my life and sweep me away in his arms.

Always blaming my weight, I never had very many boyfriends. After one failed engagement, the dream of the prince, white horse, and happily-ever-after quickly dissolved into the reality of needing a job. And, get a job I did — not just any old job. No, I got a job where I witnessed happy couples every day, embarking on a new chapter in their lives together through engagement and marriage. I worked for a large jewelry chain, selling engagement rings as their primary profit-making product. But, instead of becoming bitter and hard-hearted, something truly magical happened for me.

I gained confidence in myself. I learned to love myself. I raised my expectations of what I thought I could accomplish, and I felt successful for the first time in my life. I worked my way up from part-time sales to supervising all the bookkeepers in the upper-half of Michigan. It felt good to be a successful suit-wearing business woman.

While the path to purpose has an infinite intelligence through which it operates, we are not always privy to what it has in store for us. We are given signs, but we don't always "get" them. I had finally come to accept myself and like myself, just the way I was, and giving up any need to have someone take care of me or validate me felt empowering. So, I stopped looking for or expecting a prince to arrive. I was my own prince, or princess as it was.

Then, just when I had aced my lesson in self-reliance, he came into my life. Just as on cue from the invisible intelligence, my prince rode in on a return sale. Instead of a white horse — a returned engagement ring delivered him to me. It wasn't my job to handle returns, but I had been trained to handle them in case the salespeople were busy. On that particular day, each salesperson had one customer in progress and one in waiting.

As I was called to the floor, I saw a cute young man waiting to be served at the counter. His name was Terry, and he had just broken up with his high-school sweetheart. Instead of a black tux and a champagne wedding toast, he got the ring back. And there he was, returning it to spend the money on some new toy: a car, a vacation, or a new motorcycle. We chatted, laughed and I flirted. Three days later, we were on our first date; three years later, we were married.

My childhood experiences in accepting others as they were and choosing forgiveness would come into play soon after we were married. An unexpected happening would cause the path to become filled with twists and turns through a labyrinth of emotions. My husband's best friend and buddy from third grade, who had been a part of our lives since our marriage, started dating my husband's former fiancé. The lessons learned from the school yard of my childhood came back as feelings swirled around the twist of fate. We either had to learn to accept their relationship or lose him as our treasured friend.

In the end, we were not willing to sacrifice the friendship cultivated through the years of their childhood together and during our marriage. We chose to accept Terry's ex-fiance in order to keep his childhood friend in our lives. Not only did I accept her — she became the best girlfriend I have ever had in my life up until that time. On their wedding day, the universal intelligence must have smiled a toothy grin as Terry stood as the best man for his childhood buddy, and I stood as the bride's matron of honor. Champagne toasts were had by all, and personally, I felt quite blessed that the universal mind that guides us on our paths had united Terry and me on the path of our future together as one. I thought the champagne tasted especially sweet that day.

Opportunities for Growth

Ouch! That could have hurt! Did we accept the lesser of two evils when we accepted and allowed my husband's former girlfriend back into our lives? Maybe that's what we thought at the time. Losing our friendship with his childhood buddy was not an option. The only way to keep his friendship was to accept his choice of a partner into our lives.

Maybe the reason for our decision was not the right one, but, it was the best one we had. With this acceptance, grudges were forgotten, resentments were released, and my husband's ex-girlfriend and I were able to start afresh as friends. Eventually, we became best friends.

There have been people in our lives that have hurt us. Some may be on your list. They may never become a friend, let alone your best friend. Nor would I ask you to attempt to make that happen. However, surprises and miracles happen when we develop acceptance of a situation, as well as, other players, and our own role in the situation.

Contemplation

Examine your list for those people who have hurt you at some time during some situation.

Action Step

Send love to every person on the list. Even if the words you are saying are hard to feel, speaking the words is a freeing action. As you read each name on the list, recite "I love and accept you just as you are."

Action Step

Notice the feelings created from the step above. Recite the same loving statement to those feelings as you did above with the person, as crazy as that may sound. Giving ourselves permission to feel whatever we feel deflates the intensity of the feeling.

"After all these years, I am still involved
in the process of self-discovery.
It's better to explore life and make mistakes
than to play it safe. Mistakes
are part of the dues one pays for a full life."

Sophia Loren

9

The American Dream

After a while, my husband, Terry and I were living what appeared to be the American dream. From the outside it looked pretty good; we owned a restaurant, a home on a lake, and two rental properties. But the view on the inside of that American Dream wasn't quite so pretty.

Things were not easy from the beginning for Terry and me. We moved in together six months after meeting in the jewelry store. Both of us were a bit hesitant about the marriage thing since we both had failed engagements. So, though we were deeply in love and talked about getting married often, it just did not seem urgent — until the universe gave us a little push, and the pregnancy test came back positive. No doubt about it; the pink cross was almost red! Through my surprise, I could almost hear the jingle from my childhood: "First comes love, then comes marriage then comes Vickie with a baby carriage." I knew that is supposed to be the order of things, but what if it doesn't go that way? What if the baby carriage happens to be a wedding gift?

Being the entrepreneurial spirit that he is, Terry had taken a leave from his job to start a printing business. I was pregnant and working a full time job. We lived in a townhouse in a rough part of town. It was so rough that there was a murder in the unit next to us! Not a great place to be poor and pregnant.

The wedding would have happened anyway. The unexpected event just moved it up by several months. My mother was a wedding planner for the church in the small town where we grew up. So, she took over, and the wedding was planned in six weeks. Morning sickness consumed twenty-four hours of my day. I was too sick to care about the details; I made the big decisions, and she made them happen. We were married at the site destined to be my parent's custom-built home. It was a small, but lovely wedding and just the way we wanted it.

Five months after our wedding, our beautiful son, Travis, graced our lives. We never regretted one moment of our decision to marry and raise our son as a family. His gifts of joy, laughter and curiosity enhanced our lives in ways we could never have imagined. I could also never have anticipated that a child could possibly be my greatest spiritual teacher.

As I entered a life of marriage and motherhood, my parents announced their impending divorce after 27 years of marriage. After many troubled years, they had hoped things would be better with retirement and a new home. But neither could erase all the years of built up resentment, fear, and frustration.

I had way too much on my plate to be emotionally overcome with their news.

The transitions were made easy through a choice to forgive, let go, and move on.

Happiness was the key and my parents were happier being apart, though there was still love between them. My mother found new love and eventually married my stepfather, a wonderful kind man who loves us as though we are his own. My ability to accept all aspects of the situation, loving them all equally, enables us to share life events as a family and has brought me enormous peace and happiness. Love is the first key to true happiness.

Terry and I never gave up on our American Dream of entrepreneurship. He went back to his paying gig, while also working at his printing business. I took eight weeks off and went back to work for two weeks, but I could not stand being away from our son. So still poor, we did something that some would call silly and others would say was downright stupid. Yet there were others who could not help but wonder how in the world we did it. We were not sure how we were going to do it either. Long before we learned that you did not have to know how to get to your dream, we just took the one step necessary towards it.

Our dream was a bright red, cedar-sided building built over a lake on pilings. It was once a bait shop and even had three row boats to rent to customers. But when we saw it, it was an ice cream and pizza shop, and we wanted it. We wanted to own it, run it, and play with it. I can not remember how we got the money for the down payment, but we did.

With a five-month-old in tow, we made it ours. It was called The Dairy Dock. We created a make-shift napping bed for Travis by placing a mattress on top of the deep freeze. The three compartment sink was perfect for his bath time. As he got older, we made roads out of homemade molding clay that he perpetually used to play with his toy cars. Customers adored him.

That same year, we bought a house on the same lake just around the corner from the restaurant. Don't ask me how we did that either. We certainly did not know how. We were learning every day that letting go of 'how' is an important step in fulfilling your dreams. How all of the pieces fit together did not make sense until all of the puzzle pieces were played. Then we could see 'the how.' We had one full-time job, two rental properties, a new business, and a run-down cottage on the lake that needed everything replaced. We didn't even have a refrigerator. We brought a Coke cooler over from the restaurant to use until we could afford to get one.

No one said it would be easy to get to your dream or that you may have to make-do being uncomfortable for a bit. New Thought Leader, Mary Morrissey says, "Don't let your current circumstances predict your future." Keep dreaming and moving forward, while letting go of 'the hows.' You have to give the infinite intelligence of the Universal Mind room to deliver your good in ways you cannot imagine for yourself. I look back now and wonder how we knew not to worry about 'the how,' and why, after all of these years, I still get caught up in 'the how' of making things happen sometimes.

Everything wasn't perfect on the path to our dreams. I worked in the restaurant six days a week and up to 14-hours a day. I brought Travis to work with me in the mornings, and Terry would come in after working a full day at his "regular" job. In addition to the restaurant and some rental properties we owned, Terry and I held the power of attorney for his father because his drinking prevented him from successfully managing his finances after his beloved wife, Terry's mother, passed away.

I would run errands and shop for supplies with Travis in tow before heading to the restaurant every morning at 10a.m. Robbing Peter to pay Paul funded our daily bread, so-to-speak, and the state of our weekly existence. Money was so tight that we decided which bill to pay by the service most threatened to be shut off at any given moment.

That our life was stressful was an understatement. More money always went out than came in. Then there were the late night calls from the rental properties with overflowing toilets or other major crises of the day. There was no peace, and certainly no quiet to be found in our chaotic existence. Surely, there had to be more to life than this. We were not sure our idea of the American Dream was what we wanted after all. But, it was what we wanted when we created it.

Pain is a teacher and always a catalyst for change. It takes difficult times to provide the impetus to look within and explore ways to improve what is not working well in our daily lives. I knew I wanted a more spiritual presence in my life, but I was still hung up on the tenets of conventional religion, which said that I was a sinner and would burn in hell if I looked elsewhere for salvation.

I don't remember when I was first introduced to Medicine Cards, a method of tarot that uses animal medicine to teach life lessons, but it launched me into a study of Native American spirituality, which I wholly embraced. The Medicine Cards just felt right to me, and they opened my mind to a spirit or higher power that was caring, loving, and comfortable. I began to care for myself and moved one step closer to understanding and honoring the Divine Essence that lies within. It also became clear that my guides and cheerleaders were grooming me to understand how to navigate the crazy, dysfunctional ways of life here on earth — like working 14-hour days, six days a week at times, with a toddler underfoot.

Opportunities for Growth

Life gets crazy sometimes. You may be in that time in your life where life is beyond crazy; where nothing seems to go "right" for you. There is always a quiet place within us to which we can turn when our world turns insane. In this quiet place, we can create our dreams by visualizing what we want in life, rather than what the reality seems to be.

You know what you want in your life, but you don't see how to get there. The path seems to have slowed, stopped, or has become downright blocked. When you are caught up in the how-to of the solution, doubt and fear only create more doubt and fear.

You've heard the scary voices—How will I get the money? No one in my family has ever done that. What am I thinking; I will never be able to do that. Your "that" could be: owning a business, going to college, running a corporation, or being thinner.

It may seem as if your friends and family are looking at your life as if they were peering into a snow globe—never-changing. In it, you would always live on the same street, stay stuck in the same rut, doing the same activities every day, over and over again. It is what they expect from you and for you.

Even though you may be living on that street in the snow globe, only you think your thoughts. And only you can change those thoughts. You can change your expectations for yourself, regardless of the beliefs you currently hold for yourself.

Contemplation

Envision a new scene in the snow globe. Make it one that you want to see for yourself in the future. Be specific. See it in vivid detail and in full color. Do not worry about how it will happen. Think only of the dream. If it requires education, you will be given many opportunities and paths to get the knowledge you need.

Action Step

When you get caught up in the "How's"—recall the scene in the snow globe that you have created. Let the worry go, and take some action. Listen to the still, small voice within, and follow its guidance. Make a call to the college you want to attend. Contact someone with the qualifications you desire, and ask them for advice.

Action Step

Repeat the action step above as often as needed until the dream is reached. Always take a step in the direction of your dreams—no matter how many times you have to remind yourself to let go of the "How's."

"Visualize this thing that you want, see it, feel it, believe in it. Make your mental blue print, and begin to build."

Robert Collier

10

Imagine It and It Will come

Through my studies of hypnosis, I discovered a technique called visualization. I was fascinated about a concept that would allow me to just imagine what I wanted—and then it would come true. It was amazing to me that we could manifest our external world by changing our inner thoughts and thought processes.

Repeating the visualizations of our heart's desires, whether it is material possessions, changes in behavior, or relationship matters; the Universe does it's magic by putting into motion the right circumstances for us to have what we desire. And it usually happens with minimal effort on our part. Some call this the power of positive thinking, but it is so much more than that.

Professional athletes often use visualization as a mental-training technique to enhance their performance. This can include imagining how the golf club feels in your hand as you swing and hit the perfect shot to the green or making successful free-throws in a basketball game. Some studies even go so far as to suggest that individuals who practice 75 percent mental training and 25 percent physical training, do better at their sport than those who devote 100 percent of their time to physical training.

Not only is this technique used by professional athletes, it can be used to great success by ordinary people to create happier and more fulfilling lives for themselves. Wallace Wattles (1860–1911), who wrote *The Science of Getting Rich*, advocated the use of creative visualization as one of the main techniques for realizing goals.

Unlike daydreaming, which is simply imagining something happening in the future and in third person, visualization is imagined in the present, and it is experienced in first person. While daydreaming is often two-dimensional, visualization often employs all the physical senses including sight, smell, hearing, feeling, and even tasting which serves to magnifies the desire and accelerate the manifestation of the desired outcome.

The favorite image hypnotists use to help others understand this visualization technique is to invite you to imagine a lemon. As you bring the lemon to your nose the sharp, fresh scent of the lemon fills your nostrils. Feel the slick and slightly bumpy surface. Place the lemon on a cutting board and slice it open. Notice how sharp and shiny the knife is and then notice how the crisp, wet smell fills your nostrils when it is released. Pick up a slice and feel the juice run down the back of your thumb. A friend nearby asks "Are you going to eat that?" Notice that your mouth is starting to water excessively, and the back of your throat is starting to pucker and ache with anticipation of the sour taste. Your neck is starting to strain with the stress.

Repeating the mental exercise of visualization every single day allows the brain to lay down muscle memory for the physical body to employ; when the resulting new behaviors are coupled with an appeal to the Universe to fulfill your deepest desire, your reality changes. This is not magic or supernatural, but simply the utilization of our innate ability to change our life circumstances through the power of our thought processes.

Opportunities for Growth

Bet it happened to you, didn't it? When you read the paragraph about the lemon in chapter ten, your mouth started to water or that stressful pucker feeling in your throat created an uncomfortable feeling. Visualization does work to create the situations we want to experiences in our lives. Athletes have been using this as one of their training methods for years with a great deal of success.

Although visualization is thought of as seeing pictures, not all of us see pictures when visualizing. Just think about the scene you are imaging, incorporating as many senses into it as you can. Use all of your senses when practicing self-hypnosis, visualizing the results of your suggestion.

Contemplation

Can you think of a time when you used visualization to achieve something you wanted? Could you see it, taste it, or feel the feelings of having it?

Action Step

Create a dinnertime story using the following five questions as a guideline. Picture that story in your mind as you practice self-hypnosis. For instance using the affirmations suggestion from Chapter Six, "I will eat three vegetables every day."

- What do the vegetables that you choose taste like?
- Can you imagine the textures in your mouth?
- Is there a scent in the room or on a person that you recognize?
- What are you noticing and seeing around you?
- What noises do you hear or conversations are you having?

Action Step

Watch yourself putting a huge amount of lettuce on your plate at your favorite buffet restaurant. You joyfully add more vegetables that you love to the plate. A touch of chicken for protein is placed on the plate. As strange as it seems, you skip the cheese and croutons, adding just a smidgen of salad dressing. When you sit at the table, you look at the plate. The beauty of the vegetables surprises you. You think, "Who knew that vegetables could look so beautiful and appetizing."

You hear your friend asking what is wrong, "You haven't even taken a bite. Are you ok?" Responding, "Yes, It just looks so good. I am glad you chose this restaurant today for lunch." The crunch of the vegetables feels so satisfying. The smell of the fresh bread is appealing but just one piece is all you want or need.

The restaurant is busy, but you are intrigued and engaged in conversation with your friend. When the meal is over, you feel happy, contented, and satisfied. Walking out with your friend, you feel proud of your choices.

"I would visualize things coming to me. It would just make me feel better. Visualization works if you work hard. That's the thing. You can't just visualize and go eat a sandwich."

Jim Carrey, Oprah Winfrey Show, 1997

1 1

Treat and Move Your Feet

Without much conscious awareness on my part, my desire to better myself was grooming me to absorb and live the principles for Science of Mind. I was creating what Science of Mind calls demonstrations. I was magnifying and manifesting my desires, not yet consistently, but I would later learn how to use a reliable scientific formula to accelerate change.

Without understanding the connection between our subconscious mind and our divine self, I yet somehow intuitively knew that our minds hold a wealth of power that we have access to. I also, innately, knew that we needed to take steps — even if they were baby steps — to realize our expressed desires. Small, seemingly insignificant actions, would ultimately get us to the place we wanted to be. Later I would learn to "Treat and move our feet," which means state your claim through prayers of intention and do something about it.

Many people will not even start taking action toward their desires for fear it will not be possible to achieve or that they will make a mistake. "It is not that we make no mistakes, but the belief in the necessity of mistakes that stays in the consciousness, and then there it is bound to be a repetition. It is our scientific practice to declare that there have been no mistakes," states Ernest Holmes.

Many people also have the misperception that huge effort is required on their part to create change. They are convinced that manifesting their material desires by altering their behavior has to be painful. Other people believe that there is a need for sacrifice or a huge leap of faith before they can reach their dreams. Holmes suggests that, "Surely there can be no Intelligence in the Universe that wishes man to be sick, suffer pain, be unhappy, and end in oblivion. Surely if God or Universal Intelligence is imbued with goodness, then It could not ordain that man should ultimately be other than a perfect expression of Life."

Personally, I found accepting the Science of Mind teachings as easy as riding a bike. My husband and I let go of our business, we took full time jobs and began turning our house into a home. We were financially comfortable, but we somehow wanted more. Our little 1,000 square foot home felt too small for our growing family.

We talked about moving to a larger home. We were ready to move, but we didn't know how we could afford to do so. Each Sunday, we would scan the real estate section of the newspaper for possible new homes in our area. As winter became spring, we began to ride our bikes through a new subdivision nearby with large new homes. As I would ride by, I would imagine what it must be like to live there. I would visualize the smell of food cooking at the kitchen stove, watching TV with my family, and I could hear the laughter as we played together in the backyard.

Did we move in the next three months? No. Six months? No. But, just about a year later, we did move to a home three times larger than the one we had. It just happened to be several states away from our place in Michigan.

The act of riding a bike through a neighborhood that I didn't really believe I could live in was the first baby step toward visualizing and manifesting a new life. The steps seemed so insignificant, yet, the result was magnificent. I had the home I'd visualized, creating wonderful family memories of the significant events in our lives.

"You never forget how to ride a bike." That's how the saying goes. You can start today to take small, seemingly irrelevant steps toward your heart's desire. Suppose you want to be a rancher, yet you live in the city. Take the simple step of searching the internet for information about what it's like to work a ranch. These days, you can probably find a video of your dream online and enjoy actual sounds of the experience. Have fun. Take pleasure in imagining yourself on the ranch even if it seems an impossible dream. It can't hurt, won't cost a dime—and who knows, you might just be putting the first baby steps in motion to manifest your desire into a fantastic reality. So hop on that bike and pedal through the desire of your dreams.

Opportunities for Growth

There is a time and place for dwelling on what is wrong in our lives. Have your pity party. Give yourself permission to feel sad, mad, disappointed, inadequate, anxious, or what ever the unpleasant feelings are. Instead of eating a half gallon of Rocky Road ice cream, smoking two pack of cigarettes, or drinking a bottle of red wine, start with using the visualization process to release the feelings.

You are already doing it; I can hear your heads swaying from side to side, "No not me," you say. When you feel anxious, what is your mind doing? Dwelling on the anxiety? Your mind focuses on what is causing the anxiety. Past events start to flash though your mind that to reinforce that you should feel anxious, or how lousy a person you are because you are feeling anxious.

The more you think about the situation, the more anxious you get. Anxiety becomes a part of life because that is what we accept it as. There are times in our lives that anxiety may be needed to make a decision about our path. However, we can flip our thoughts and visualize the favorable outcome we desire.

When our son turned 16 and started driving on his own, I was fine until his curfew was coming up, and he was still not home. Lying on my side, facing the bedside alarm clock, I gazed into it like it was a GPS and would tell me where my son was and when he would be home. Pictures of deadly car wrecks flashes through my mind. It was like I was watching a newscast. The images were quite graphic, detailed, and colorful. In my minds eye, I could see the crumpled Jeep upside down. The firefighter used the jaw of life to cut open the Jeep while it caught fire. Screaming teenagers lye on the ground, bleeding profusely. I heard the ambulance arrive at the scene. EMT's rushed to the scene, putting the injured in the ambulance. The police directed a medi-flight helicopter to land on the road as one of the teenagers (I am sure it is my son) is placed inside and flew away.

My mind races: How will I find him? How will they know to contact me? How bad is it? Is he alive?

My heart felt like it would jump out of my chest. The anxiety levels soared through the roof until I could no longer bear it. Who would I call first; the police, hospitals, his friends?

Then I heard a sound. My son's Jeep pulled in the driveway.

All of that worry for nothing—thank goodness! He was safe. He had always been safe. After a couple of nights with this scenario, I realized it was a waste of my emotions and my time—not to mention my lack of sleep.

Changing the visualization, I could go into a restful sleep without the worry and anxiety.

This is how the new visualization progressed:

It was based on a gift from my mother to help me be more aware of my driving habits. She presented me with a visor angel carrying the words, "Don't drive any faster than your angel can fly."

As I was lying in bed, I would imagine my son's angels and guides helping him to make wise decisions, staying focused on his driving, and providing a protective "bubble" around his Jeep. I visualized him being attentive to the road, his surroundings, and how the Jeep was handling. I could hear his friends talking to him, yet he still kept his eyes on the road. I saw him waving to his friends as he dropped them off at their homes, calling out some rude comment that teenage boys find funny with a shout-out as he drove away,

"See you at school on Monday." I imaged the angels and guides instructing him and guiding the Jeep home. I would pray for his protection and safe return. After turning it over and letting it go, I awoke only to hear the Jeep pull into the driveway.

When you find yourself using your powerful mind to conjure up unfavorable outcomes, start visualizing the outcome you desire rather that dwelling in the feeling or situation of worry.

You will find that you shift on many levels emotionally, physically, mentally, energetically, and spiritually.

Contemplation

Think of a time when you worried unnecessarily about a situation in your life. Write down how you handled it. What did you do to make the situation worse?

How did the situation turn out?

Action Step

What visualization could you have used to lessen the burden? Be specific and write out how you would use your new knowledge about visualization to handle the situation better and with less anxiety.

"When one door closes another door opens; but we so often look so long and so regretfully upon the closed door, that we do not see the ones which open for us."

Alexander Graham Bell

12

Let It Go

When you are a young adult, you often feel that you are supposed to be suddenly in control of your life. The statement, "Let Go and Let God" was nothing more than a string of words to me. I was probably still a little angry from previous religious experiences and probably a little presumptuous that I could handle everything that was thrown my way. After all, I was an adult!

I continued to seek spirituality and a greater understanding of the world, but I was convinced that I was in charge of my life and my child's life and I certainly wasn't ready to trust God to take care of me or my family. I kept hearing about letting go and letting God—but what did that really mean? Did it really mean to just let go and not have any control and no worries … wasn't that a cop out? Wasn't I expected to have responsibilities, especially now that I was an adult?

So, life (and God) decided to show me what letting go was all about. I learned how letting go can help you get what you want, and then some. Wayne Dyer talks about finding peace, noting in his book, *Being in Balance*, that "peace demands heroic thinking and a purity of conscience." It would be a long time before I really — in a deep, spiritual way — embraced the peace that could be obtained by letting go.

We still owned a small restaurant but needed additional income to make ends meet. I was lonely, bored, and needed to get out of the restaurant world. About this time, I was presented with an opportunity to work in the local University bookstore during their back-to-school rush. It would only be for a week or two, but I was desperate to do something different. We would probably lose money because I would have to hire a baby sitter and someone to take my place at the restaurant. But it didn't matter. My emotional health depended on it. I was hired as a cashier working a register for up to eight hours a day. And I loved it!! It was fast-paced, and I could talk with the incoming students. I made new friends with the staff. It was a totally different environment than the one I was used to being in; one where I spent most of my days entertaining our toddler between customers and being very bored.

The job of Head Cashier caught my eye. She was in charge of scheduling the cashiers and taking care of the registers. I remember looking at her one busy afternoon as she addressed the needs of her staff while at the same time taking care of a couple of problems with the registers. I could suddenly see myself doing her job and I knew I could do it well. As fast as I thought the thought, I dismissed it. How could that ever happen when I had a full time job at the restaurant?

That same year, the University's football team made it to the Rose Bowl. The bookstore needed someone to run a makeshift souvenir store, and when it was offered to me I jumped at the chance. We had already decided to close our restaurant for the winter, so I was available.

Suddenly I had a purpose, and I was so happy. The head cashier and I became very good friends, and all the managers loved me and my work ethic. I was in heaven. Then something unexpected and amazing happened. One of the buyers announced her retirement, and they needed a replacement. My friends and managers on the staff encouraged me to apply, and I did so without hesitation. Within a few short weeks, I had a job that I loved and would never have imagined for myself. My title was Concession Store Buyer, and I was working for a Big Ten University. Wow—what a shift in my reality! I went

from being a bored and lonely mother and restaurant opera-
tor to thinking "I want her job" to actually having something
so much better! Ultimately I became the General Merchandise
Buyer for the entire store and was responsible for all emblem-
atic and soft goods. In essence, I bought everything but the
textbooks.

It all happened, because I was able to "Let Go and Let God."

It wasn't a totally smooth ride; there was another candi-
date they were seriously considering for the job. But it was
really more than I'd ever imagined for myself, and it all happened with very little struggle or pain.

I also experienced another letting go moment with the
restaurant. Terry and I reopened it that spring while holding
down two full-time jobs and parenting our pre-school son. It
became overwhelming and exhausting. So we gave it back to
the owner we were buying it from. One day I just knocked on
her door and handed the keys of the restaurant to her. Then I
turned around and walked away. How amazingly freeing that
felt. It wasn't without a hiccup or two … she sued us for the
remainder of our contract, but in the end she was able to resell
the property with the improvements we'd made, and it was a
win-win for everyone.

Yes, there were setbacks along the way to achieving such
remarkable results. But in hindsight, the remarkable lessons
in detaching from the fear and the results, with far greater
rewards than imaginable were well worth it. Letting Go and
Letting God isn't just a saying—it can be your reality!

Opportunities for Growth

Yes, there were setbacks along the way to achieving remarkable results. But in hindsight, the lessons learned in detaching from the fear and the results with far greater rewards than

imaginable were well worth it. "Letting Go, and Letting God" isn't just a saying—it can be your reality!

Setbacks, fear, exceptions and regrets keep us "stuck up." We stay paralyzed in this mode as if we are trapped in a cage. You still may be stuck in a cage with some of the ten people on your list, unable or unwilling to turn towards the open door because we are angrily or mournfully looking back at the closed door.

The key to the cage is a beautiful and often misunderstood word--forgiveness. Many believe that as you engage in this activity, it pardons the persons or situation because we do not see their actions reconciled by taking responsibility for them If we don't forgive them, it feels like we are making them pay for what they did to us. Unfortunately, it is far from the truth. Keeping this resentment is only hurting us more. It is what keeps us stuck. We have always held the key to get out of the cage. It was our responsibility to turn the key.

Maybe you have heard this before. Perhaps you have not been ready in the past to embrace it. If the situation you desire is not manifesting, then you may want to at least consider doing your forgiveness work.

Forgive. Forgiveness is the courage to say, "I am precious and valuable enough to move on. Whether anyone else takes responsibility for their actions or not, I love myself enough to take charge. I have given away my power to them for too long. It is my turn to be set free from now on."

It feels easy to say the words of forgiveness, but do you believe them? If you don't as yet, you can.

Contemplation

Choose a person on your list that you need or want to forgive.

Action Step

Prepare, as before, to practice hypnosis. Before you recite your suggestions, picture in your minds-eye a lovely park setting such described below.

The temperature is perfect for you. Feel the warm sun and the cool breeze against your skin. Imagine the flowers, trees, fountains, creeks, and walking paths. You choose a place to sit and soak in the calm, peaceful surroundings. A figure approaches you. You feel safe, as if you know them. You recognize them as a person that you respect for their wisdom and power. They can be someone you know—family or friends. They could be Divine—angels or Jesus, or a contemporary figure of respect, such as Eleanor Roosevelt or Oprah.

They sit next to you take your hand and nod. It is understood that they are there for you. They are your support team and will give you strength. They look deep into your eyes, and you feel a calming power transform you.

They inform you to look forward. Sitting at a comfortable distance the person that you chose on your list is sitting front of you. They look a bit confused but receptive.

You start first. "I forgive you. I release the power you have kept over me."

They just sit looking at you.

You continue, "More importantly, I forgive myself for giving you my power; for being in the wrong place at the wrong time; for making it all my fault; for letting this go on for so long."

Add other thoughts or feelings you have about your self in the situation or with that person that needs to be forgiven.

When you are done with your list, say to your self and the other person. "I set you free. I set myself free. I am forgiven."

They turn and leave you. The person of wisdom and power holds you close. You are free. You have always been forgiven.

Peace is yours.

"Our intention creates our reality."

Dr. Wayne Dyer

13

So, Where Is Here?

Intention is setting a specific outcome by identifying a desired result and magnifying it through a conscious thought process. As an example, before attending a speaking engagement, I set an intention to meet two potential clients and sell ten self-hypnosis CD's. And sure enough, that is exactly what happened. Conscious thought energized by the power of intention produced results.

However, there have been many events in my life that produced results that I did not consciously set in motion. It's not that I didn't have the intention, but I did not combine it with the conscious thought process. My studies have helped me understand that our thoughts are our reality. I believe that somewhere in my past, I set into motion events that led me directly to Science of Mind. I don't really know whether it was a conscious decision, or its genesis. It may have come from my distrust and disdain for conventional religion that had me taking baby steps into awareness of other spiritual options. But, the result is that I'm here now.

When did my first step onto my path to purpose occur, I am not exactly certain. Was it through the pain of being overweight that caused my parents to put me in front of teachers who increased my awareness of new ways of thinking? Was that what I chose my particular parents to assist me with in this lifetime? We can only speculate the whys and hows of our lessons here. What I know for sure is that without my knowledge, understanding, or awareness, I was gently being groomed for Science of Mind.

As a newly minted hypnotist, freshly certified and eager to learn more techniques to help others; I collaborated with a colleague and she recommended two books to me. One of the books she used with her clients, and the other book she used personally. The first book was *You Can Heal Your Life* by Louise Hay and the second book was *The Emergency Handbook for Creating Money Fast* by Carol Dore. I adore both of these books, and I credit Louise Hay for so positively changing and healing my life. It was not until several years later, while I was attending Science of Mind classes, that I discovered both authors are Science of Mind Practitioners. Hmm, I have to wonder if that was a set up for my path.

A few years back, I was looking for a way to help my husband bring some clarity to his life, so we signed up for a workshop. It was a fun group with varied activities designed to help us to interact with different attendees at the workshop. While we specifically attended the workshop to help my husband, it was me that ended up receiving help.

At the conference I was introduced to an interesting woman and was intrigued by her studies in Natural Mysticism. I made a mental note to ask her to have coffee with me to hear in greater detail the course of study she was pursuing. Not too long after the workshop, I found myself sitting across from her at lunch. We talked about Natural Mysticism and Science of Mind. I was fascinated and enthralled, but just knew I was way too busy to attend a weekly class. I let it go and put the thought out of mind.

However, the Universe had other ideas and a short time later a client talked to me about a class she'd just been to earlier that week. She mentioned how fun it was and how the discussions were on target for her life. So, my curiosity got the better of me, and I called the instructor who happened to be the woman I had met at the workshop! "Lisa, I know you have already started your classes, is it possible to still join?" She replied, "Of course you may, and I look forward to you attending next Monday."

I could not wait for Monday to arrive. I wasn't sure what to expect, and it was with some apprehension that I walked into the space at Inner Peace that Monday evening. The uneasiness dissipated within the first hour. I felt like everyone was talking a language that I had never heard before, yet somehow understood. I was relieved to find a space where I could just be me. Whether I was wearing my "speaker clothes" or sweat pants, I was accepted. I just knew that I could say whatever I wanted without being judged.

The most surprising reaction was that I felt like I was home, deep inside I was comfortable. It was like a veil had been lifted, and I was remembering again who I was and where I came from. From the first day of class I knew — just knew — that I was in it for the long run. Staying the course for three years to obtain my practitioner's license? You bet. Two more years of Ministerial classes to become licensed? Not a doubt in my mind.

My left brain was thrilled to learn that Science of Mind is based on a scientific formula of prayer. "Treatment is the time, process and method necessary to the changing of our thought," said Ernest Holmes, founder of Science of Mind. This definition rang true for me. Just like in the practice of hypnosis, treatment alters our thought to produce the change we choose to see in our lives.

I always felt the spiritual relationship through hypnosis, yet I never completely understood the connection to Spirit. The practice of treatments provides the bridge to the practice of hypnosis and spiritually. Ernest wrote that, "Treatment is clearing the thought of negation, of doubt and fear, and causing it to perceive the ever-presence of God."

My belief that we all have a power within us was validated when I learned that "we see that we have within us a power which is greater than anything we shall ever contact; a power that can overcome every obstacle in our experience and set us safe, satisfied, and at peace, healed and prosperous in a new light and a new life." –Ernest Holmes

This power within is the individualized use of Universal Mind or God. Treatment sets the Holy Spirit or Law of Mind into action. "Whatever goes into the subjective state of our thoughts tends to return again as some condition." Ernest Holmes. Therefore, we are the results of our own thinking.

WOW! These were all concepts I agreed with and had been groomed for. And it was unbelievable, yet fascinating, to me that these truths are held in a religious philosophy. I may have felt like I took the long way, but I knew I was home.

Opportunities for Growth

I am.

Begin paying attention to how many times you use the statement "I am" during your day. Whether you are just thinking it or saying it out loud it counts. While you are observing: notice how you are using the "I am statement." Is there a negative affirmation after it or a positive one? What is the percentage of negative to positive?

The statement "I am" is extremely powerful. Words create energy. It describes what you set as the intent for the moment, even the entire day. It defines our world and our place in the world. It gives you a label for others to use to define you.

It goes deeper than that. The "I am" statement is a hypnotic suggestion. Every time the subconscious mind hears those words, it works to make the intention set by them happen. That's right; whether it is detrimental or kind, the subconscious mind says "Ok, so It is." Let me show you that is who you really are.

These words are also a Divine Expression of the inner "I AM". Some religious groups and theologians believe that I AM is a name for God.

Every time you start a statement using the words, "I am" an energetic frequency is created, putting into motion through Universal Law your intent to create a new you or immobilize the current you.

Contemplation

How many times a day are you saying to yourself something negative? Are you involving your inner "I Am"?
For example:

I am stupid.
I am tired.
I am fed up.
I am overwhelmed.
I am not enough.
I am not smart enough.
I am not good enough.
I am so fat.
I am so ugly.
I am lazy.
I am a procrastinator.
I am unproductive.

Feel how just reading those statements can create a low-sinking feeling? That happens even if you don't believe them to be true.

Action Step

Repeat these statements:

I am happy.
I am smart.

I am energetic, vibrant, and excited.
I am relaxed and calm.
I am competent.
I am enough.
I am great at figuring it out.
I am confident and powerful.
I am precious just as I am.
I am beautiful and valuable.
I am industrious.
I am eager and excited.
I am a productive and organized.

How does that feel? Notice how much better you feel, even though you may not believe the statements yet.

Action Step

To get unstuck in a jiffy, notice how you are using the statement "I am." Reframe the negative statements to positive ones. During your self-hypnosis sessions, visualize your positive "I am" statements as actions. Send your prayer to the Divine, knowing with complete certainty that your request will be answered.

"The trouble with our praying is, we just do it as a means of last resort."

Will Rogers

14

A Treatment to Practice

This Prayer "Treatment" consists of five relatively simple steps. Follow these steps to turn your situation around. You are more than a product of your conditions.

1. **Recognition**
   Give your source of power a name. It can be God, Mother, Father, Universe, Source, Great Spirit, Great Mystery, or J.I.M. (my husband's name for God, 'Just Intelligent Manifestation')

2. **Unification**
   The knowing we are one with the One. We have never been separated from God but are living examples of God. Divine in our nature, we are loved for doing nothing more than breathing. Just that alone has fulfilled all of our obligations to God. We are precious, deserving, and worthy of the GOoD that we are.

   I remember hearing in traditional Sunday school that we are all children of God, but that held no meaning for me until I understood from the principles of Science of Mind that I am not only the child of God, but rather a part of the Divine, living the earth plan. Because I am part of it, some say I am a co-creator, while others simply say I am the creator. Either way, I already am everything I want to be, therefore I can have whatever I want to have.

3. **Declaration**
   In this step we claim what we desire. No more begging, pleading or negotiating with God for what I want. Because I am a co-creator and part of God, I simply claim my desires. At first, many people claim material items such as parking spaces near the front door or all the traffic lights to turn green when late for an appointment. Later we realize that we want more than what those things will give you. What we are really seeking is peace, happiness, satisfaction, and joy.

4. **Gratitude**
   Giving thanks for what we already have is one of the highest forms of prayer. When we review what we already have or how far we have come on our journey, a shift occurs in our minds and bodies. We become more relaxed, more content, and more satisfied.

5. **Release**
   Just let God take care of the details. This can be the most difficult step in the prayer. Often we want to be in control. After all who better to stay on top of a situation than the one who knows it best? However, it is not until we surrender or let it go and let God figure out the details that the prayer treatment works. God will bring people, places and events into our lives that we could never even imagine by ourselves.

Through the study of Science of Mind, I have accomplished goals I would have never imagined possible. Being a minister and a speaker would not have even entered my conscious mind when I was asked as a child "What do you want to be when you grow up?" I now have more amazing, caring, and loving friendships than I have ever known in my life. More importantly, I have found myself. Using the prayer treatment daily I have discovered the peace and prosperity I am meant to have.

Have you ever seen the T Shirt line where stick figure people are hiking or biking? The slogan on the shirt says it all:

"Life is Good
or is it Life is GOoD?"
And So It Is.

Opportunities for Growth

Prayer treatments are ways to forgive any remaining misgiving that you have for any of the people on your list. You are treating for YOU and your benefit—not to change them. Treat for any hurt, regret, guilt that keeps you stuck.

Contemplation

Are there lingering issues that you have for anyone on your original list of people? Consider those you would like to heal your feelings about.

Action Step

Performing a prayer treatment is easy. Just follow the steps below.

Step one - **Recognition**
This is an easy one. What do you call God?
Heavenly Father

Step Two - **Unification**
Announcing and reminding yourself that you are one, with and of God:
"Breathe through and for me as I rest in the knowing that I am of the Divine. I have never been alone for I am always a part of you as your child. And, just like any parent, you carry me when I am afraid, comfort me in my sickness, and cherish me as precious. Because I am your child, I am one with you at all times."

Step Three - **Declaration**
What do you want? Announce your desires in present tense just as Jesus did:
"I claim and declare peace. I release any limiting beliefs with grace and forgiveness, which I have created. I enjoy daily confidence, vitality, and strength—mentally, physically, and emotionally. My relationship with our family and friends grows deeper and more loving everyday. I choose for my life and my work to be easy and prosperous. Abundance of wealth is accumulated everyday and flows through me. I am healthy. My body understands and reflects the spiritual wholeness that I am. Choosing to eat nutritious foods and exercising is easy for me."

Step Four - **Gratitude**
"I am grateful for these gifts. I am grateful for the healing, prosperity, and grace that fills my life everyday."

Step five - **Release**
"I release this treatment into the Divine Word, understanding and knowing that "It is done," just as it was promised onto me.
And so it is.
Amen.

You are **Ready**. The tools have placed you on **Set**, now **GO**! Use these tools to change your thoughts to produce the positive outcome you desire.

Epilogue

A woman sits at a computer for hours, busy handling phone calls, texts, and emails as a new word document is opened. As she sits facing the words before her that represent her life, she contemplates, "Should I or shouldn't I?"

Some have said, "It's too personal, it is all about you." Others have read the document, and said, "You have to; it will inspire others to take action."

She types as new words come to her mind, and she strains to hear the whisper of the inner voice of the Divine. She knows the voice, the small non-judgmental influencer that nudges her forward, even when it is scary. All the lessons from the years of preparation come flooding in from her heart mind. Feeling afraid is just a perception, a thought. She remembered: Change the thought, change the outcome.

Just in that moment, the words of the voice became clear and concise,

"You are ready, you are set, now go."

Are You Ready to get Unstuck?

Review of Action Steps

Chapter One

Make a list of the ten most important or memorable people who have impacted your life.

Chapter Two

1. Look at your list from Chapter One. Write the one word beside each person that describes the primary feeling you had as a result of your experience with them. Write one sentence describing the belief about yourself that your experience with that person confirmed.
2. If the belief that you developed in the exercise above is a negative one, write down a positive statement that you would rather believe about your self. It is okay if you don't believe it is possible for now. On your journey through reading this book, you will discover how to make the changes necessary to erase those old daunting belief systems so that you are using the Law of Cause and Effect to your advantage.
3. Read the positive statements you have affirmed every night just prior to sleep to reprogram your subconscious mind.

Chapter Three

Acknowledge your feelings about your list of ten people. Are you still mad, sad, or resentful? Do you feel guilty, want to blame them, or _____ _____ (insert your feelings here)? It is perfectly okay to have those feelings.

Chapter Four

Make a list of five habits you would like to release. What emotions do they evoke? How is your habit serving you now?

Chapter Five

List one meaningful example in your life of a way that someone on your list knocked you off your path to create a new one or make you more determined to stay on the path you where on?

Chapter Six

Practice self Hypnosis at least once a day for 30 days. Pay attention to your behaviors and your thoughts. These changes may be so subtle and easy that you may not have noticed them.

Chapter Seven

Look into your eyes in the mirror and say to your self, 'I did the best I could, given the time and circumstances in my life. I deserve to feel loved, precious, and valued. I love you."

Do this three times a day, always looking in a mirror. Say this affirmation lovingly to the child within the person looking back at you and mean it.

Chapter Eight

Action Step: Send love to every person on the list. Even if the words you are saying are hard to feel, speaking the words is a freeing action. As you read each name on the list, recite "I love and accept you just as you are."

Action Step: Notice the feelings created from the step above. Recite the same loving statement to those feelings as you did above with the person, as crazy as that may sound. Giving ourselves permission to feel whatever we feel deflates the intensity of the feeling.

Chapter Nine

Action Step: When you get caught up in the "How's"—recall the scene in the snow globe that you have created. Let the worry go, and take some action. Listen to the still, small voice within, and follow its guidance. Make a call to the college you want to attend. Contact someone with the qualifications you desire, and ask them for advice.

Action Step: Repeat the action step above as often as needed until the dream is reached. Always take a step in the direction of your dreams—no matter how many times you have to remind yourself to let go of the "How's."

Chapter Ten

Action Step: Create a dinnertime story using the following five questions as a guideline. Picture that story in your mind as you practice self-hypnosis. For instance using the affirmations suggestion from Chapter Six, "I will eat three vegetables every day."

- What do the vegetables that you choose taste like?
- Can you imagine the textures in your mouth?
- Is there a scent in the room or on a person that you recognize?
- What are you noticing and seeing around you?

- What noises do you hear or conversations are you having?

Action Step: Watch yourself putting a huge amount of lettuce on your plate at your favorite buffet restaurant. You joyfully add more vegetables that you love to the plate. A touch of chicken for protein is placed on the plate. As strange as it seems, you skip the cheese and croutons, adding just a smidgen of salad dressing. When you sit at the table, you look at the plate. The beauty of the vegetables surprises you. You think, "Who knew that vegetables could look so beautiful and appetizing."

You hear your friend asking what is wrong, "You haven't even taken a bite. Are you ok?" Responding, "Yes, It just looks so good. I am glad you chose this restaurant today for lunch." The crunch of the vegetables feels so satisfying. The smell of the fresh bread is appealing but just one piece is all you want or need.

The restaurant is busy, but you are intrigued and engaged in conversation with your friend. When the meal is over, you feel happy, contented, and satisfied. Walking out with your friend, you feel proud of your choices.

Chapter Eleven

Action Step: What visualization could you have used to lessen the burden? Be specific and write out how you would use your new knowledge about visualization to handle the situation better and with less anxiety.

Chapter Twelve

Action Step: Prepare, as before, to practice hypnosis. Before you recite your suggestions, picture in your minds-eye a lovely park setting such described below.

The temperature is perfect for you. Feel the warm sun and the cool breeze against your skin. Imagine the flowers, trees, fountains, creeks, and walking paths. You choose a place to sit and soak in the calm, peaceful surroundings. A figure approaches you. You feel safe, as if you know them. You recognize them as a person that you respect for their wisdom and power. They can be someone you know—family or friends. They could be Divine—angels or Jesus, or a contemporary figure of respect, such as Eleanor Roosevelt or Oprah.

They sit next to you take your hand and nod. It is understood that they are there for you. They are your support team and will give you strength. They look deep into your eyes, and you feel a calming power transform you.

They inform you to look forward. Sitting at a comfortable distance the person that you chose on your list is sitting front of you. They look a bit confused but receptive.

You start first. "I forgive you. I release the power you have kept over me."

They just sit looking at you.

You continue, "More importantly, I forgive myself for giving you my power; for being in the wrong place at the wrong time; for making it all my fault; for letting this go on for so long."

Add other thoughts or feelings you have about your self in the situation or with that person that needs to be forgiven.

When you are done with your list, say to your self and the other person. "I set you free. I set myself free. I am forgiven."

They turn and leave you. The person of wisdom and power holds you close. You are free. You have always been forgiven.

Peace is yours.

Chapter Thirteen

Action Step: Repeat these statements:

I am happy.
I am smart.

I am energetic, vibrant, and excited.
I am relaxed and calm.
I am competent.
I am enough.
I am great at figuring it out.
I am confident and powerful.
I am precious just as I am.
I am beautiful and valuable.
I am industrious.
I am eager and excited.
I am a productive and organized.

How does that feel? Notice how much better you feel, even though you may not believe the statements yet.

Action Step: To get unstuck in a jiffy, notice how you are using the statement "I am." Reframe the negative statements to positive ones. During your self-hypnosis sessions, visualize your positive "I am" statements as actions. Send your prayer to the Divine, knowing with complete certainty that your request will be answered.

Chapter Fourteen

Action Step: Performing a prayer treatment is easy. Just follow the steps below.

Step one - **Recognition**
    This is an easy one. What do you call God?
    Heavenly Father

Step Two - **Unification**
    Announcing and reminding yourself that you are one, with and of God:

"Breathe through and for me as I rest in the knowing that I am of the Divine. I have never been alone for I am always a part of you as your child. And, just like any parent, you carry me when I am afraid, comfort me in my sickness, and cherish me as precious. Because I am your child, I am one with you at all times."

Step Three - **Declaration**

What do you want? Announce your desires in present tense just as Jesus did:

"I claim and declare peace. I release any limiting beliefs with grace and forgiveness, which I have created. I enjoy daily confidence, vitality, and strength—mentally, physically, and emotionally. My relationship with our family and friends grows deeper and more loving everyday. I choose for my life and my work to be easy and prosperous. Abundance of wealth is accumulated everyday and flows through me. I am healthy. My body understands and reflects the spiritual wholeness that I am. Choosing to eat nutritious foods and exercising is easy for me."

Step Four - **Gratitude**

"I am grateful for these gifts. I am grateful for the healing, prosperity, and grace that fills my life everyday."

Step five - **Release**

"I release this treatment into the Divine Word, understanding and knowing that "It is done," just as it was promised onto me. And so it is.
Amen.

You are **Ready**. The tools have placed you on **Set**, now **GO**! Use these tools to change your thoughts to produce the positive outcome you desire.

About the Author

Vickie Griffith is the owner of BreakThrough, www.BreakThrough.org, a company she began in 2000 to empower women during the healing process from a variety of painful situations. Her compelling, genuine, and humorous methods of demonstration give others the tools they need for making immediate and positive change.

Griffith's passion for helping others stems from the astounding results she has experienced with Hypnosis, EFT, and the Science of Mind Principles. Utilizing all of these gentle, safe, and effective techniques, she has accomplished seemingly impossible personal goals, including the release of over 49 pounds, which she has kept off for years.

Researching methods of complementary healing arts since 1976, Griffith holds a Bachelor's degree in Management and Organizational Development from Spring Arbor College in Michigan, and is currently an adjunct professor at the University of Richmond, Virginia. She is a certified Hypnotist from the National Guild of Hypnotists, is a EFT (Emotional Freedom Technique) Professional, and a Science of Mind Minister.

In addition to coaching and mentoring, Vickie Griffith is a speaker and a writer. She conducts workshops on the topics of Creating Balance, Stress Management, Eliminating Self-Sabotage, and Money Magnetism.

She lives near Richmond, Virginia with her husband Terry, their two rescue-turned therapy dogs, Surrey (Australian Koolie) and Sparky (Australian Cattle-Dog Mix).

To add fun, inspiration, and motivation to your next event—contact Vickie today! She is available for group and corporate speaking, individual consultation, and phone sessions.

Get a free report on the Five Words that Hinder Healing at http://www.break-through.org/5words.html